D1135359

ILLUMINATED
MANUSCRIPTS

ILLUMINATED
MANUSCRIPTS

BROCKHAMPTON PRESS
LONDON

THE HOUSE BOOK OF CERRUTI,

Italian, Verona or Lombardy, late 15th Century

The sections on sanitation and medicine in the house book of Cerruti are a Latin version of an Arabian health text. This illumination provides a detailed depiction of a lemon tree and a basil plant.

The illustration continues the lineage of the monastic herbaria, (manuscripts with pictures of herbs) which in turn reflects the significant role ascribed to herb gardens throughout the Middle Ages for both medicinal and culinary purposes.

A GREAT NUMBER OF the most creative works of art to survive from the Middle Ages (c. A.D. 1000 - 1500) are found in illuminated manuscripts. In much the same way as today a poet and an artist might collaborate upon an illustrated volume of poetry, so in medieval times the illuminated manuscript was the product of a partnership, between a scribe (or scribes) - who wrote out the text - and the illuminator(s) - the craftsman who produced the images. However, as the printed press was not invented until the Fifteenth Century, the entire medieval project was manufactured by hand.

The illuminated manuscript was an extremely costly commodity to produce. With paper only scarcely available until the Thirteenth Century, manuscripts were usually fashioned from sheets of animal hide, known as 'vellum'. Vellum was produced through a process of soaking, stretching and scraping the skins of either a cow or a sheep. When these skins had been cut down and gathered together as pages for a book, the scribe was able to begin inking in the text. As he did this, he made sure to leave spaces at the points where the illuminator was planning to supply decoration. This could be in any of three places in the manuscript: in large initials beginning a passage of text; in the margin; or lastly, in partitioned partial or full-page picture spaces, called 'miniatures'.

The word 'illumination' was initially used to describe the light effects produced by the gold used by illuminators in their decoration, now it is taken more generally to refer to the ornamentation of a manuscript. Gold was in fact only one material employed by the illuminator, and his skills needed to be not only those of a metal worker, but also of a draughtsman and a painter. When his ink sketch had been finalised any metal work planned was begun, either laid on as leaf, or in a gum solution applied with a brush. The final stage of illumination was reached with the introduction of colour in opaque, egg-based paints worked up from dark through to light.

Until the Thirteenth Century the monasteries were almost the sole producers of illuminated manuscripts. The majority of these works were large religious books such as Bibles and Bible commentaries intended for corporate use, either in the liturgy, or in monastic libraries. From the Thirteenth Century on, the rise in universities as centres of learning and an increased urbanisation led to a more diverse patronage, which in turn led to the production of a wider range of book types and subjects, both religious and secular. In addition, there was an increase in texts written in the vernacular and picture books began to be produced, in which the illustrations were granted primacy over the text.

The unique selection of images from some of the world's great libraries presented here explodes the myth of civilisation abandoned in the so-called 'Dark Ages'. For it captures instead the vivacity of a medieval culture presented with astounding beauty in the intricate artistry of the illuminated manuscript.

igitur clementas

'KING LUDWIG'S MISSAL' French, 13th Century.

left A missal is a manuscript which contains all the texts required for the celebration of the Mass. This illuminated initial depicts two symbolic figures: Ecclesia - the Christian Church - on the left; and 'Synagogue' - the Jewish faith - on the right. As Synagogue's crown and tablets fall to the ground, the image celebrates the primacy of the New Testament and of grace over the Old Testament and the law.

ANTIPHONARY OF BEAUPRE, **Belgian, 1290.**

left An antiphonary is the liturgical book which contains those parts of the Mass or the monastic Divine Office which are sung antiphonally (i.e. in responses) by the choir. This particular folio (or page) contains the antiphony for Easter Sunday, and divided within the initial 'A' are illustrations of the resurrection and the three women at the tomb. The two figures kneeling to the left reflect the devotional nature of this subject-matter.

LIVRE DU ROY MODUS ET DE REYNE RATIO
French, 14th Century.

overleaf This is a good example of the type of manuscript produced for secular patrons at this time. It is a history book, and the miniatures reflect the courtly passion for hunting. The illustration has been marvellously schematised into an ornamental pattern, which remains extremely easy to read, and which may be dramatically contrasted with the perspectival approach adopted in the Tres Riches Heures less than a hundred years later.

a qui la beste uendra doit estre de
ceste contenance. ¶Il doit mestre
son arc au lonc de soi et la main
de qui il tient la corde de son arc

or turer sa seestr nielques au fer
doit amisti. por tenur son en
s et asseer sa main et laissier
er. Et se la beste ment a roi

GRADUAL OF SIENA CATHEDRAL, Siena, c.1473.

right A gradual differs from an antiphonary in that it has those hymns sung after the Epistle during the Mass. The artist of this example is known to have been Girolamo da Cremona, a man obviously employed by the Sienese to produce an object which would boast of the wealth of their cathedral. The musical score has noticeably become subservient to the rich illumination which includes within the initial 'R' scenes of Christ risen, and the soldiers at the tomb; and in the medallions events from Christ's life.

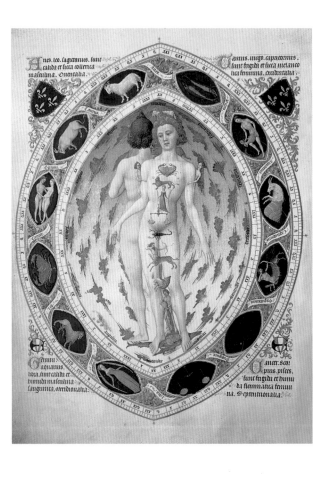

LES TRES RICHES HEURES DU DUC DE BERRY
French, c.1416.

left The calendar tables in the Riches Heures are followed by
a chart depicting in a mandorla (an almond shape) front and
rear views of a man, framed by the anti-clockwise cycle of the
months of the year and their accompanying star signs. This
belief in a relationship between the parts of the body and the
signs of the zodiac originated in Hellenistic-Roman astrology
and continued almost unaltered through the Middle Ages.

Les Tres Riches Heures du Duc de Berry, French c. 1416.

right The calendar illustrations in the Riches Heures are startlingly innovative in their approach, with a full-page miniature provided for each calendar month, the labours of the month painted occuring in nature, and with the establishment of an illusory pictorial depth. This painted miniature is the calendar illustration for the month of October, and in the background we see the Gothic Louvre, the most lavish structure of its type at this time.

The Travels of Marco Polo, French, 1375.

overleaf This late fourteenth-century miniature from France pictures a scene from Marco Polo's visit to the Kubilaj Khan in Peking, and shows the Khan raising taxes on salt, spices and wine. His court is described through a wonderful use of lateral perspective, presenting a walled exterior jutting out to the right, with a door through which we visually enter into the court interior.

SCIVIAS, Hildegard von Bingen.

right This full-page miniature illustrates the sixth vision of Hildegard von Bingen - a Benedictine nun and visionary who lived in the Twelfth Century. Here, her vision is of heaven, an image presented in the rationalising manner of a diagram, with circular rings partitioning off the various heavenly creatures.

YEAR AND CALENDAR, French, 1460.

overleaf The twelve labours of the month are here grouped together in a miniature sectioned into twelve. Such calendars commonly appeared in Books of Hours, devotional manuscripts which provided a yearly structure of prayer for either a lay or clerical reader.

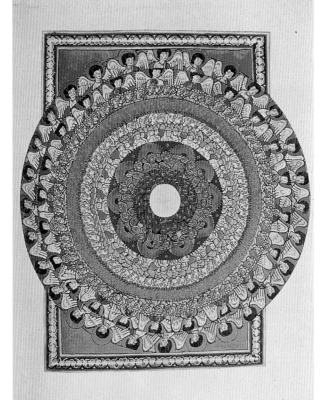

CODEX MANESSE, Zurich, c.1310-1340.

right A beautifully illustrated collection of courtly poetry, the Codex Manesse projects the romance of Germany's feudal system in the Fourteenth Century. It is a history conveyed through verse, and here the theme of love continues with Jakob van Warte - identifiable through the heraldic devices of his shield and jousting helmet - quite literally waited on hand and foot by several anonymous, but well-dressed ladies.

Codex Manesse, Zurich, c. 1310-1340.

right A miniature by a different artist from previous Codex Manesse page. The image presents an idealised picture of courtly life, in which the notionalised natural setting forms the platform for a detailed description of the colourful trappings of a knightly existence. The heraldry of the shield and helmet identify the knight out hunting with a falcon as Wernher von Teufen (doc.1219-1223).

BOOK OF HOURS OF CHARLES D'ANGOULEME,
French, 15th Century.

left This miniature employs a carefully structured
composition to give stability and legibility to a very lively
theme. The picture may be divided vertically into three with
the music and dance of a party taking place in the foreground,
whilst in the middle region shepherds are just visible on the
hills overlooking a city, as an angel lights up the sky at the top.
Much of the appeal of this treatment of the Christmas story
lies in the artist's sense of observation, recording the festive
customs of the time - which included the playing of bagpipes
(on the bottom right).

YEAR AND CALENDAR, 16th century.

right The month illustrated is that of August, and the accompanying labour, wheat harvesting. The subject-matter of the labours has, as in the Riches Heures, become just one element in a wider, seasonal depiction of an inhabited landscape. The use of perspective and the inclusion of an artificial, metalwork window frame place the emphasis very much upon the thrill of illusion.

COMMENTARY ON ISAIAH, German, c.1050.

left The dynamic, wide-eyed figure style of this illumination announce it is one of several Ottonian manuscripts executed by an artist/scribe called Liuthar. In this instance we have a commentary on Isaiah, and the scene depicted is that found in Isaiah chapter 6, with the prophet taken up into the heavens, where a seraphim lays a live coal on his mouth to purge him of his sins.

veugleux est priua
cion de la veue. vn
bomme est priue de
ueue. au tunie sfois
n deffaulte de lœil et de la punielle ou

BARTHELEMY L'ANGLAIS, LIVRE DE LA PROPRIETE DES CHOSES, French, 15th Century.

left This manuscript illuminates a French translation of the English friar, Bartholomew's popular late medieval anti-ecclesiastical writings. The artist would appear to have drawn inspiration from everyday sights in picturing the scenario of a blind man being led precariously across a bridge. The blind man is a musician, and the attention paid by the artist to his hurdy gurdy is further testament to the role of music in medieval life.

LES TRES RICHES HEURES DU DUC DE BERRY,
French, c.1416.

right This folio constitutes the calendar illumination for the
month of December. In the foreground two types of hound
and their handlers surround a captured wild boar. This is an
adaptation by the artists - the Limbourg brothers - of the
usual illustration for this month which commonly showed the
killing of the fatted calf. The precedent for the Limbourgs
chosen subject-matter is thought to have come from Italy,
where the artists may well have travelled.

reſchier fils tout premiere
ment te renſeigne que tu ai
mes dieu ton ſeigneur de
tout ton cuer. ⁊ de toute ta
uertu car ſens ce tu ne puez eſtre ſauue.
Item tu te don garder de toutes les choſes
que tu ſaies deſplaire a noſtre ſeigneur
ceſt de tout pechie mortel. Et plus deuoi
es ſouffrir quel en te commentaſt de tout
martirie que faire aucun pechie mortel.

HEURES DE LOUIS DUC D'ANJOU, **French, 14th Century.**

left The duc occupies a huge bed with voluminous, white sheets draped around him in angular, creased gatherings. A poet cuts across the fleur-de-lis patterning of the canopy to present Louis with a manuscript. The miniature is bordered by a foliate design in which exquisitely rendered birds perch, among them a jackdaw, a green woodpecker and a magpie.

DU BOISROUVRAY PSALTER.18. FRENCH, **c.1260 Amiens.**

overleaf The two minatures reproduced here come from a full prefatory cycle illustrating Christ's life. As New Testament illustrations accompanying the Old Testament book of Psalms, they depict the prophetic interpretation of this text. On the left, Christ is pictured before Pilate, whilst below Judas expresses his regret, on the right are the interment and the resurrection. Note in particular the characterisation of the Jews, all of whom wear pointed hats.

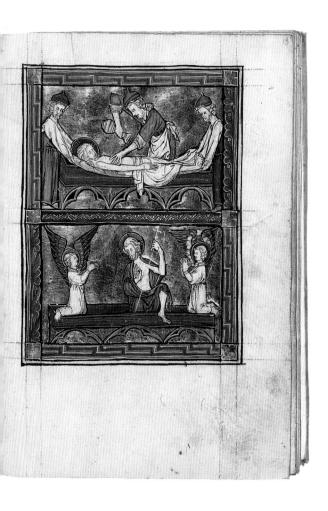

CALENDAR WITH ILLUSTRATIONS OF THE MONTH,

Flemish, 16th Century.

left The month of June is associated in this late Flemish calendar with the tournament season - a wholly secularised and urbanised approach to the genre. The town has been taken over by the event, and even scaffold stands have been erected for the sizable audience.

BEDFORD HOURS, French, 1423.

overleaf The diptych miniature for the month of July has as its subject-matter a harvester and the star sign of Leo. This is a simpler, more condensed approach to a calendar than that found in the Riches Heures, and the illumination provides a clearly visible example of brushed gold work applied in thin strokes over the paint surface.

Commenten memoueque aua

ar le dit nulius rparat must en e

car fist le kalendier ce moys lui est a
nacer lez moys de lan q̃ estoiet cõfus es ka

GRANDES CHRONIQUES DE FRANCE, French, 1375/79.

right This tightly patterned miniature uses a dissection of the picture space into two to tell the before and after of a story. In the top half, John II, the Good, King of France (1319-64) grants the Order of the Star to a fraternity of knights templars who are found banquetting below. The 'Grandes Chroniques de France' were written in 1375-79, and this version was copied out for King Charles V.

Coment le duc de lancastre et le duc de
bretaigne vindrent a paris pour eulz col-
lenant le roy. mais le roy pust le fait
. . . L len. quil en sa man .
. . . . nus cens cinqate deux .

dicte bataille. le Sire de Briquebec. le chas-
tellain de Beauuais pluseurs autres no-
bles tant du dict pays de bretaigne come
dautres mauldis du royaume de france
. . . tem. en icelu an . . ccclix. le mardi

pres le trespassement du roy phe se-
saloys regna pour luy Jehan son ainf
ne filz et fut couronne en leglise de

CHRONIQUES DE SAINT-DENIS, French, 15th Century.

left The artist responsible for this miniature is known to have been Jean Fouquet. A painter not only of manuscripts, but also of large panels, Fouquet is but one example of the links between the arts which existed right through the Middle Ages. His mastery of portraiture and his familiarity with Early Renaissance developments in Italy are both exhibited here in a miniature depicting the arrival of King John the Good and Joanna of Boulogne in Paris after their coronation in 1350.

VISION OF ST HILDEGARD, c.1230.

right The first half of the 13th Century was a time of growing popularity in apocalyptic and visionary texts, works which appealed to a desire to interpret the times and to a curiosity about the unknown. This miniature abandons perspective in order to illustrate two intangibles: Hildegard having a vision (bottom right), and the mystical content of her revelation.

PICTURE CREDITS

First published in Great Britain in 1997 by **Brockhampton Press**
20 Bloomsbury Street, London WC1B 3QA
a member of the **Hodder Headline Group**

© Brockhampton Press, 1997.

ISBN 1 86019 487 7
A copy of the CIP data is available from the
British Library upon request.

Designed and produced for **Brockhampton Press**
by Keith Pointing Design Consultancy.
Text written by Robin Plummer MA

All images courtesy of AKG London.

Printed and Bound in Italy by L.E.G.O. Spa.